The Presence of Things You Cannot See

Alexandra Wynn

BookLeaf Publishing

India | USA | UK

Presentation by *BookLeaf Publishing*

Web: www.bookleafpub.com

E-mail: info@bookleafpub.com

ISBN: 9789357747943

First edition 2023

To the struggles that I overcame and the experiences that I could only process in words.

The Presence of Things You Cannot See

There's a pocket of warmth in the middle of this air-conditioned room.

Cloudy condensation dances off the surface of the table. Making an invisible presence known.

A silent whistle only the dog can hear. Traveling at a frequency beyond what eyes can comprehend. His pointy ears perk with diligence.

A tickle of the nose, from inhale to sneeze, Microscopic particles travel from a forgotten corner through nasal passageways. Riding the wave of lungs pulling air in and out.

This room vibrates with the presence of things we cannot see.

The Ceaseless Climb

And the world said "You don't belong here, I
don't want you, I want better."
"But I want better too," she said.
And she took another step in blind faith towards
the light.
And the world said "I don't want you" a little
louder but she kept on walking.
In a retaliative roar, the world yelled "I DON'T
WANT YOU" and made her ground unstable.
The rocks became slippery, the sand became
quick, the waves became menacing.
The light brightened to reveal its pull on others
so far ahead of her.
And no matter how close she got, she couldn't
feel its warmth on her skin.
Her voice a distant whisper to the others ahead
as she begged them not to leave her behind.

So she drove her heels down harder with each step forward, not knowing what else to do but to climb ceaselessly against the current.

Cherry Blossoms

The way they open to the sun is as natural as the smile it brings to my face. Bursting through to meet the clockwork of April. A swarm of pink bending to the mercy of the wind. Vibrating to the limits of a two-week life span. No room for anything but life at its fullest.

Cotton Candy Clouds

Bubble gum pink against the cerulean sky. The sun reflects off dispersing clouds to create cotton candy pillows delicious enough to eat.

So this is where NY hides its sweetness. In the early daybreak hours, in the space between the closing clubs and morning shifts.

So this is where NY hides its peace, away from the demands of the bright sunlit day, away from the fear of the dark cold night.

Suspended in a confetti-colored sky. Fleeting and teasing, like the last bite of dessert.

Sunsets

There's comfort in knowing that evening after evening you see them too. That the brilliant glow that warms my face tonight is the same one that bounces off the freckles on yours. As if distance doesn't matter at all.

Red Red Wine

Timeless. Rich. Burgundy bliss.
Tip of the tongue tang.

Gurgling free from the bottle.
Swirling round a crystal dome.

An evening treat that travels to the unburdening
mind. Tempering muscles. Allaying the day
away.

A Love Letter to Sisterhood

We grew up in a world that didn't see much light
So we became the light for each other
Responsible, soft, fiery, and spirited
Contrasting personalities that came together to
build a sisterhood that transcends compatibility
The laughs are as loud as the yells, the cries are
as savage as the accomplishments
Every day is a work in progress, but everyday
we rest in the tranquility of each other's support
Our mother had nothing to give but love and
perseverance so we do our best to take her lead
and help her with the rest
It's not only blood that bonds us, it's the desire
to see and be seen and a decision to love
unconditionally

You Took The Life Right Out of Me

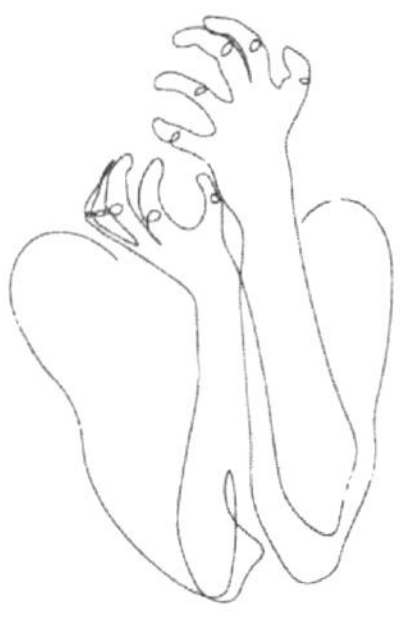

You took the life right out of me
You didn't even let me see
Or say goodbye or plant the seed
I trusted you knew what was best for me
But you buried the lead
So you could proceed with a fleeting pleasure that
only met your needs

You said don't wait too long
After I danced to the tune of your song
But it didn't register to me then
When I didn't even have a boyfriend
That it meant loneliness for eternity
Didn't even know what it would take to build a
family

And now I have no choice

No breath of hope
No boundless bundle of joy
Because you played with my body like a toy
And took the life right of me
Before I could even see
How much it'd mean to me
How much I had to lose
You robbed me of my right to choose

Where should I go

Where should I go
When I've been everywhere
but belong nowhere

When I've basked in awe at wonders with new
friends
Only to go home to meals alone and languid texts
from old friends

When I have piles of business cards that stack higher
and higher
Responses as elusive as a ghost,
illusive as a good first impression,
allusive as the unsaid goodbye.

Where should I go
When I've seen everything
but reflect nothing.

Wishing the world was a mirror that wondered at me
the same way I wondered at it.
I've exchanged thoughts in many languages and
kisses with attractive faces
I've heard foreign music that elated my soul

And yet I'm suspended in space
with no will to surrender to the gravity of a
permanent place

Restless

It's like grasping for something mid-fall and failing.

It's like a thirst unquenched. A wound unhealed. A scale unbalanced.

It's knowing there's more just beyond your reach.

A Break from Heartbreak

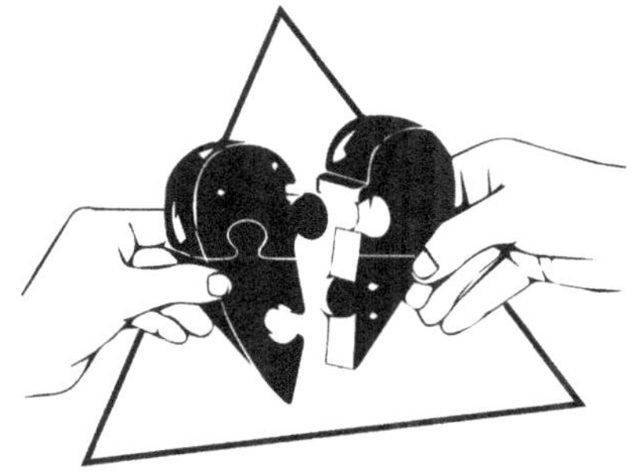

Every second that I'm not thinking about you is a glorious moment.

A precious relief where my breath comes naturally and tears aren't scratching up my throat or burning at the insides of my eyes.

Where my chest has space to balloon and my skin is goosebumpless.

A peaceful space where I can safely be me. The me before I met you.

The Beginning

Everything shines a little brighter in the beginning. Adrenaline runs a little higher in the beginning.

Craving layered kisses one on top of another. Never wanting the rush to end.

Every word is politer. Every thought a selfless tribute to love. Your happiness is my happiness. Entwined is where I want to be.

What I would give to stay in the beginning. To lengthen the distance to the middle. To keep the ending out of sight. To stay at the head of the long hilly road of love.

What I would give to avoid the rotunda. To stop
going round in circles, avoiding exits like red
flags, until I have no choice but to find the one
that takes me back home alone where the ending
meets the beginning to start all over again.

No Need For Checkmate

For the first time, there are no games.
Every other time was a vicious chest match
Longing for a checkmate, an end to the battle
A calm to my overbeating heart.
No more fear and adrenaline from the fight.
When you say you want me there, I believe you.
When you sigh with comfortable pleasure, I hear
you.
When you say I miss you, I feel you.
And I want you to feel me too.
I want you to reach for me in the middle of the
night and I know I'm there.
I want us to retire our chest sets for good.

The Extended Hug

Imagine a stronger feeling to the one you get
from a hug
One where you can melt in the natural furnace of
body heat
Where you can entwine your leg with his…
comfortably guided by the nooks and hinges of
thighs, knees and ankles
You place your head on his chest and you can't
tell whether the pulse in your ear is his or yours
Breathing in sync with that one vein you can
visibly see pulsating
Chest hairs tickle your nose as you bury your
face in them
You softly stroke the back of your fingers
against his opposite arm
Slipping down down until he catches them in his
Entwined fingers and arms join entwined legs in
an unfurled hug that heals the soul

Embarrassed

Base of throat closed
Skin hot to touch
Tunnel vision
Heart-rate high
Shallow breath
Paralyzed voice
Brain racing with thoughts
Wait, what do you mean?
Oh no, did that just happen?
What do I do next?
Get me out of here
Automatic apologies
Emotions shutting down
Unconsciously ignoring the world around me
Trying not to see shocked or annoyed faces
Blocking out negative comments

Pretending it didn't happen
It didn't happen
It didn't happen
What just happened?

Seasonal Depression

I open my eyes to familiar walls that have no
light bouncing off them
Alarm blares over the sound of another day's
boundless rain against the window
Pressing snooze to prolong the start of its
vivacious-less hours

Feeling captive and cornered, pacing between
two constricting rooms
No incentive to step out with gritted teeth and
bare knuckles against the frigid wind
Knowing that the tantalizing air against my skin
and filling my lungs would be better than the
stagnant one inside
But the lifeless concrete view outside my
window says otherwise
So I sit on my couch in paralyzed indecision
longing for sunshine, nature's motivation

Of a Certain Age

Creaky knees like old door hinges.
Snap crackle pop at the slightest movement.
Veiny hands that don't lie, betraying my
youthful energy, revealing my unwanted
wisdom.
Saggy breasts that fill bigger and bigger cups,
Bra holding them up to where they used to be.
Stubborn belly fat below the button.
Thankful that most asses have stretch marks too.
Hair thinning. Lost to the shower's drain.
Nails brittle. Breaking at the slightest touch.
All physical signs of aging. And yet why do I
feel like I'm saying goodbye to a part of myself
that is not just physical?

World, Can You Stop For Me?

The world spins too fast for me to keep up. I have this hope that every new experience will lead to something wonderful but it never does. What is it about me that repels progress and belonging? What is it about me that loses steam so easily? At the first sign of adversity. I used to have so much perseverance. Am I really just so tired? How do I become untied? Where do I get the energy to barrel through and run at your pace?

Mornings on the NYC Subway

The hoards of people shuffle impatiently towards the subway door - unable to wait the seconds it takes between the train stopping and the doors opening. My face comes inches away from others shuffling out as they instinctively head towards the stairway to transfers, escalators, and exits. I take advantage of any piece of space I see, entering the open subway doors and beelining for a vacant seat. Damn, the old Asian lady gets there first with such lighting fast skill and precision unbecoming of her old age.

The Great Relief

The greatest relief I have ever known is when you said there's no more you or me. There's only us.

www.ingramcontent.com/pod-product-compliance
Lightning Source LLC
Chambersburg PA
CBHW070731160726
48003CB00006BA/2452